12.95

soul data

Previous winners of the Vassar Miller Prize in Poetry
Scott Cairns, Series Editor

1993   *Partial Eclipse* by Tony Sanders
        selected by Richard Howard

1994   *Delirium* by Barbara Hamby
        selected by Cynthia Macdonald

1995   *The Sublime* by Jonathan Holden
        selected by Yusef Komunyakaa

1996   *American Crawl* by Paul Allen
        selected by Sydney Lea

SOUL
DATA

soul data

poems by Mark Svenvold

Winner, Vassar Miller Prize in Poetry, Heather McHugh, Judge

University of North Texas Press
Denton, Texas

Permissions:
University of North Texas Press
PO Box 311336
Denton TX 76203-1336
phone 940-565-2142
fax 940-565-4590

To contact author for readings, send email to Mark Svenvold at:
mail@wylieagency.com

The paper used in this book meets the minimum requirements of the American
National Standard for Permanence of Paper for Printed Library Materials,
z39.48.1984. Binding materials have been chosen for durability.

Library of Congress Cataloging-in-Publication Data

Svenvold, Mark, 1958–
    Soul Data / Mark Svenvold.
        p.   cm.
    ISBN 1-57441-046-6
    I. Title.
PS3569.V48S68   1998   97-39406
811'.54—dc21   CIP

Design by Accent Design and Communications

A c k n o w l e d g m e n t s

Special thanks to Scott Cairns, Janie Geiser, Sarah Chalfant, Paul Hunter, Stephen Thomas and Peter Stitt.

Grateful acknowledgement is made to these publications, where the following poems first appeared:

The AGNI Review: Eternity, A List; Trees and November; Desperate Message (Exigencies of the greenback hold)

The Atlantic Monthly: Erosion

Fine Madness: Bad Dates: An Excerpt from the Anthology; The Predicament of the Virtuoso (Monk As Midas)

The Gettysburg Review: I [In this rain, then]; II [Noir]; V [Linoleum]; VI [The Buffalo Shoe Factory]; VII [Cloudy Bright]; VIII [Picaresque at the Cabaret Hegel]; IX [Demolition]; X [How then begin, how to answer]; Relearning Winter; Variations on a Theme by Stevens

Lullwater Review: West Oakland Somniloquy

The Nation: Villanelle *Fin de Siecle*

New Letters: Augury; Winter Solstice; Variation on the Theme of Disappearance; Player Piano (Crows At Dusk)

Point No Point: Alfalfa; Blue Monk

Ploughshares: Graveyard Shift; Postcards and Joseph Cornell

The New York Times Book Review: Desperate Message (Their hands have found)

Under 35: The New Generation Of American Poets: Tiny Histories; Desperate Message (When the jets crowd close); Desperate Message (Their hands have found); Desperate Message (Not the end of the world)

The Virginia Quarterly Review: Variations on Themes by the Doors; Work; Poverty Music

C o n t e n t s

THREE: Notes and Elegies

for Martha

Strange and hard that paradox true I give,
Objects gross and the unseen soul are one.

—*Walt Whitman, "A Song for Occupations"*

A l f a l f a

The aging yet unhittable knuckleballer
contemplates the nipper at the plate—

he of the ka-jillion dollar contract,
(and latest pierce in pate, in scrot-)

and still a veritable embryo in socks.
Youthful offender. Finicky nemesis.

*

The old necromancer lets loose
a harvest fly across the grassy isthmus

of Oklahoma: lazy as a nosebleed, a breeze
rippling the cattle pond like incoming negligee . . .

from several levels of remove—
(field to word, soul to tongue)

the unthreshed, unbroken code
of arrival, of regard . . .

ONE

Death of the Cabaret Hegel

I [In this rain]

In this rain, then, in a fallow field at dusk,
sloped to a forest edge, the seen-through
sorrels the deer melt from and into,
a wind works. Trees like angle iron in a brisk
April gale—a crow flares then sets upon a husk.
Now at least we see what does what to whom.
But of the *ad hoc* hopeful, the quick and new
cadences, the green upshot through brush
and all the rest, the *moon-June* sluiceway
of shades and in between subaltern greens—
that canopy of dazzlement? *Forget about it.*
But you can't, your sentences a leafing out, a *resume,*
the air like silk drawn into the lungs,
the milkweed hillside sleek as belly velvet.

II [N o i r]

A week's worth of good weather, the holiday
birders gone, the shell toss game extended,
(first lob then wobble then soft, one-hand
clap on taupe-colored sand) makes it Monday,
noon, with Philip Marlowe squinting in a tatty
darkened room once slept in by a president
(*Madison?*) whose white wig hangs suspended
like some booming brontosaur,

                       bereft of the parade.
How the cloud does nothing, sets nothing aright,
yet looms, then resembles, then resolves
our larger puzzle into page-flutter—tweety-bird
tee shirts & trampolines & somebody's great-
great-uncle's Abraham Lincoln trinket—
that's what he's after, and before:

                              (*shimmer and dissolve*)

III [M a r l o w e]

Between the deliberate surf and the hasty guess,
news comes, but only as a rumor in the trees.
The slant light and tremor of August continues,
in its soft slide, its benign aimlessness,
to beg the question. Do we decide, or does the bus
just come, the rumbling *machina* in the *deus*—
and we get on, *decided*, delivered from sleep
or versions thereof: the fine mess
whelming over the breakwater, dinner done,
the body gurgling, order restored in the provinces?
The ocean does the oceanic thing,
you know, lying low, and won't let on.
Marlowe knocks one back, a casual gesture—
the bed a shuttle of repose, of erasure.

IV [West Oakland Somniloquy]

As the sun sets the body becomes liquidier,
until in darkness all is sloshing and carryin' on,
the body's jellies a prelude to the sobbing that's to come—
but what of it? That's the way we like it here,
a steady rain stipulating the water,
constancy copied and dopplered into open
space, like a promise or premise to build upon.
It's the nothing come of nothing that we're after.
And if a duck or two float by, caviling, messing
with the program, it's only fair.
Soon enough we're back into our weather.
Our voices laid out, mad-cap, unspooling,
take the shape water takes, or air,
all echo—no *here* here, no *there* there.

V [Linoleum]

South of Spokane Street, a gear works
turns its teeth—shadows in a cavern,
through the cycles of a drop-forge piston,
heft themselves and recoil in a dark
rain of sparks, the echo off the blocks—
pa-tang!—arriving late, repeats itself again,
a ceaseless, a remorseless hammering home,
a point made and lost in the patterns of work.
Across the street, a hunkered stretch of houses,
swing sets and cyclone fencing, a klatch of cars.
The agent shrugs—"It's zoned Residential/
Light Industrial"—*pa-tong!* A lunatic fringe
of gladiolus fronts the walkways and the rows
of empty rooms we roll by at low idle.

VI [The Buffalo Shoe Factory]

They made a line of boots for lumbermen—
steel-toed homely things, hobnailed
& treble-stitched along the outer welt,
high-topped, a yard of lacing to the shin,
the rust-brown tongue a supple, second skin,
the rest as stiff as sheet iron. The tread grabbed—
you could walk up the side of a house, it seemed—
they were ugly boots you'd bet your life on, or in,
if that were your lot—but it isn't, of course.
Yours is a thrift-store scene, an antiquarian's
eye presiding over whatever's left
of the world these boots are stand-ins for.
And bowling shirts, their names slant-stitched,
are castoffs you try on, laughing, for a fit.

VII [Cloudy Bright]

You lived there for a sense of scale,
the factory gutted—just you and its square footage,
like a giant companion, more like acreage,
you said, the light rolling over the *schola*
cantorum you built with your carpenter's hands—
a bay view, half-loft, a half-darkened stage,
or era. The town faced a continent's western edge
that the *Bill Shively Band* might yammer & wail,
it seemed, and poetry happen. Malarkey, too,
those twin drunks applauding in the corner,
joined, as always, by the hip: we were all
prop wash and sputter and cool remove,
while you wore the mirrors, and stared
us down, and ranted, and climbed the walls.

VIII [Picaresque at the Cabaret Hegel]

The angel-haired one spoke in semaphores
above chantey & anchor clank,
though by then we'd lost our chantey and our clank.
The sea, alma mater, Doing Business As
Almighty Obstacle, withheld the shore,
bete-noired us something serious & we drank
our hopes & thumped, bumped bottom. We drank,
& gathered and made noises with our mouths:
"The angel-haired one spoke," etc.
                              Then a breeze,
by god, conspired & winked us forth
into some elbow-swinging song, the weather fair—
phosphor the color of bottle glass on wave caps,
hull spray like some Pentecostal glossolalia,
all glister & excess, all foolishness—
                              unless you were there.

IX [Trees and November]

We call the dead — they answer.
We call the living — they do not answer.

Then the wind picked up and moved out,
taking all we had promised. Our conspiracy—
something out of nothing, a leaf of thin air—
was now wholly air, whispering *oh,*
by countless numbers, *oh, we've done it again.*
It's true. We'd gone and done it again.
The wind blew. We hurled ourselves about
like bad dancers, embarrassed by the scene—
my favorite month, they'd sigh, *the leaves and all.*
Let's face it, they were falling apart.
It wasn't meant to be, we said, in our way,
but what, really, could one say?
That, for a while, we did what we could do?
(Our memory was good. We knew what we knew.)

X [Demolition]

Late between sets, on a fire escape
that darted six floors down and swayed
to the slightest breeze, half-baked in the halyards,
we'd trade lines and tote the night's mishap.
Meanwhile: the barges ploughing the strait
headed out, and as guys who got paid
good & regular watched what they made
spread in chevrons, the iron-plate,
stern-coughed waves of their passage
a kind of past that lay before them,
visible, rearward, so the future at their backs
makes a ghost of me still, idling here
at Sixth and nowhere. And the freeway, overhead,
roaring, won't say what it is or what it lacks.

XI

How then begin, how to answer
the red brick in a red brick pile,
bulldozed in the bright light of day, & all—
the truck-stop waitress at the coffee counter
saying *C'mon. Get it together,*
with a wink and a nod and a smile
straight from purgatory? I'll sleep awhile.
I'll lay me down and sleep the winter
squalls away. I'll grow an adipose fin
and burble in the water table some dim
little song in Chinese & see what happens.
I'll get it. But for now the astronomer walks
the asymptote and fiddles with all the clocks—
a leaf falls, and the sharp air sharpens.

Relearning Winter

Hello Winter, hello flanneled
blanket of clouds, clouds
fueled by more clouds, hello again.

Hello afternoons,
off to the west, that sliver
of sunset, rust-colored
and gone too soon.

And night (I admit to a short memory)
you climb back in with chilly fingers
and clocks, and there is no refusal:
ice cracks the water main, the garden hose
stiffens, the bladed leaves of the rhododendron
shine in the fog of a huge moon.

And rain, street lacquer,
oily puddles and spinning rubber,
mist of angels on the head of a pin,
hello,

and snow, upside-down cake of clouds,
white, freon scent, you build
even as you empty the world of texture—
hello to this new relief,
this new solitude now upon us,
upon which we feed.

Variation on a Theme by Stevens

Time favors the durable forms.
The rest the wave wash sustains
in promissory notes, a hereafter
in the click of rocks,
in the susurations of the sea grass.
At tideline, the beach tilts familiar underfoot,
hard and compact, one of the forms.
Above the beach, in a pasture
not ours, but one we've snuck onto,
one as big as the state of Connecticut,
it seems, yet still admitting of the stars,
come evening, and for all that
thick with Indian pinks and bee balm
and a little yellow flower called
butter-and-eggs, the air smells so
of sweet corn & onion grass
that one would want to interject
upon the crickets, to trespass
and comment on the *just-washed air*
to the stranger in the Savonarola chair,
some platitude or other—
and fall back from the venture,
not to defeat
but to some other sort of silence.

*

Two crows hop in a fresh-mowed field.
Another chough in a tree
talks to itself like a deaf old man,
beyond the rigamarole of means and ends.

15

TWO

After "Mr. Lucky," by Henry Mancini

Villanelle *Fin de Siecle*

—At the Dia Center for the Arts

The empress fiddles with her dress—
Outside, champagne apostles canter and enthuse.
We've reached the end of something I would guess.

Here's a man, alone, a work in progress,
a performance piece called *Man Alone In Warehouse*.
The empress fiddles with her dress.

He reads a book, his jaw clenched in earnest
hauteur, as if to pause would mean to choose
not to reach the end of something, I would guess.

Move closer: he works a red-hot wire to trace
each line, which darkens, browns, and burns, of course,
(of course), as the empress fiddles with her dress.

Each line, every word . . . he's paid to erase
by the hour. We approach by silent ones and twos
to watch—*what?*—the end of something? And who would guess

the wild, cropped mane of a beautiful empress
would carpet this landscape so, to muffle the news?
The empress fiddles with her dress.
We've reached the end of something I would guess.

Poverty Music

Full moon and a siren wailing,
the freeway a quarter-mile off,
somnolent, never sleeping—half a cigarette gone,
when up the steps she comes
in search of an edge, the world
a verb in her throat: she is small,
her coat the color of sandalwood, and she weaves
her length in and out the wrought-iron railing
pleasurably in silence,
eschewing the hand's advance,
showing a sensible mistrust of smoke,
then gone, caught up in her urges, her brief visitation
accomplished the way, tonight,
high-school kids with their throaty automobiles,
down some stretch of backroad,
in one, long diminishing harangue,
say so much with so little.

*

The world gives up its ghosts,
which walk among us and are us—
neighbors arranged in separateness,
stacked three-high in brown stone,
the rough traffic of days we think we enter
when it's all an elaborate *adieu*,
a leave-taking allowed for and forgotten,
like the *it* in *it's snowing*,
spoken casually, yet beyond dominion . . .

*

I saw a crack of it, blue,
then the deeper ether.

•

Blue Monk

Here come your many-colored kites
on a sorry little wind. They twirl and spin.
They say, who needs the wind
when the rhythm section's right?
On the radio, I hear Job's expatriate
sideman, amok in flower-beds and fruit-stands,
troubling the doormen of Fifty-second again.
You played the same tunes each night,
but laid them sideways, -ur this and ersatz that.
Who but you knew what you meant?
And in your room, that mirror above the piano—
twirl & spin, what did you see in that?
Tough task, to be crazy *and* right, and even you didn't
quite get it, flat-fingered, picking the lock to *Just a Gigolo*.

The Predicament of the Virtuoso (Monk as Midas)

Soon we grew tired of all the vouchsafing.
We considered (from a distance)
his last moves, a cautionary progression—
his wife, his mistress, his dog.
Amid this golden host
the eye craved the ordinary,
a fork, a glass of milk, ordinary things
began to leap out in relief
like idle girls discovering their coy surfaces—

Midas sat, swallowing his own spit,
while the world capered about, untouched.

E v i d e n c e

Now that the light has fallen, and the leaves—
and the sky a grey-green picture tube—
now that the sky has slowly, inscrutably, fallen,
and the many—look at us with our select
bottles of wine, our movies on video tape
and our blankets; now that we huddle warmly
in the dry corner of a rented house, poised
against a new era with its solemn belchings forth,
I think of you, Thelonious—
who so effortlessly didn't give a fuck,
who to spite those who knew music
and despite the rest, the weary, teary lot,
their faith high on a pillar
stuck in the middle of a harbor,
the madonna of liberty blessing
even their grandstanding, unctuous, capering
howdy-dos from presidency to presidency—
how you gave your testimony,
taught us a lesson in liberty—
how most of us have used ours up and carry
what's left as we carry our bodies,
pouting and untenable, from place to place—
how you charted, in short-hand, how it was then,
down on the street corner, mid-century—
how one foot, one chord, one word, one note
can still miraculously follow the other, even here,
deep within the shadow of doubt.

Variation on Themes
by The Doors

—The Comet Tavern, Seattle

The kind of grey I mean involved an envelope
of cloud cover: boyhood enthusiasms, blue
enthusiasms, and others; and a war whose fire
burned like some Kentucky mining tragedy,
& found an afterlife in a deep seam & just
burned, baby—and fueled by no wind

but a certain dark bitumen, burns still, beyond the wind's
scope—and no sealed shaft, no crucible or envelope
of black-marbled descent will heal or make it just.
And thus the living face the kind of blue
entente the living make, and shrug off tragedy.
On the turnpike, the tunes turned up, *Light My Fire*

arrives on its knuckles—*not my fire,*
man, but hey, they cooked in their time—and the wind
blows over Babylon in a late style of tragedy,
with its blur, its grey, grand envelopment,
unpinpointable agency, harum-scarum & boo-hoo blue,
nothing new—just a bit harder to tell what's just,

just a bit harder to care what's just
when you're strange, young & wasted—when Fire
and Brimstone gods of Empire in blue
serge suits scoot beneath a make-shift wind,
survey some scene's sorry, enveloping
aftermath, unforeseen for some grey reason, *tragic,*

well, yeah, we'll say in bars, knowing tragedy,
without form, without style, becomes just
a version of the kind of grey I mean, an easy envelope,
my only friend, the end, etc. And the world lies down in fire,
and the world rises up again, my friend—out the window—
the kids are coming, and they aren't singing the blues.

The kids are coming—black-booted, blue-eyed,
baby-faced & beer-fisted, untouched by tragedy,
though they've come tonight like the wind
between storms *(take my yoke upon you)* as the just
have always come, in fear, in phoenix fire,
(learn of me) in search of something to envelop

—but I digress. The night's blue lights envelop
the day's below-the-fold tragedy, and the fire
the wind whips then sweeps away is final, and just.

S t o r y

—the leap over the rail make do as the squeeze between

wrought-iron shop doors meant

to keep *them* out;

as copped and robbered as one can;

as gangly as the body when for real and for keeps is;

as graceless & choppy & breathless &

full of moves
as cops can't catch is—

stuff, junk, loot, shit—

giddy from the chase, from the sheer high

order of gun metal

breached there (the footage of it, open

ended as it is)—his

moment under the sun,

in broad daylight—

(equals *something something something*

with a byline,
what

we'll make of it)—

newsrooms hip-deep in the business,

(giddy) concern, a piece of the corpus,

the face

of a boy, now positioned, toggled, *stet*—

now double-clicked in

typeface—

SAVE'd, flicker-flashed, dispatched

it

feeds

the wire.

W o r k

The garage lit by a solitary bank of lights.
Enough to work by, a dingy light—
green on green enamel cinder-block,
rows of blackened windows high-up.

Static and fuzz—the knob on the radio
broken off, the radio smudged with finger-prints, grease.
Where the knobs should be, brass shafts, cloven.
The delicate positioning fingers do with a dial,
thumb and fore-finger
starting a nut on a thread.

Bins filled with bolts dark from use,
heavy bins you couldn't lift, bolts to pick through—
flat-washers the size of coins, lock-washers, clipped
for torque, for a firm seat, a future.

Out of the box, out of the wrapper,
heavy in the hands, a clean part is a thing to behold—
it will shine, it will fit.

A bottle appears—*MacNaughton's.*
We've worked a double shift,
and like a kid with a secret
he says, as if inviting us to a party,
let's do another eight.

In the silence that follows,
a long, off-the-air silence, I shiver once
and do another eight.

The New All Girl Anal

Work, it seems, the having to be there,
happens on grey Mondays with cases of fire retardant
especially & for instance, dropped by the pallet-load
head high and sidewalk deep,
a half-block maze of boxes stacked
against passersby who side step
or slide through grim with personal injury
and also with blazers and pigeon-colored ties.
And right about 10:00
the Soho model from upstairs is pulled too fast again
across the cobblestones by the golden lab
on a leash to its piss place.
Soon Lester from Will Call will, finally,
with his head through the Will Call slot,
survey the gridlock & clamor hemorrhage
of taxi horns trumpeting the ascension of *I say so
but I'm fucked while I'm standing here*
and with his blown out mouth
say *let's go girls*, and there I'll be with my hands
professional saying, midstreet, in traffic,
c'mon back, c'mon back, c'mon back, jackass,
to the mirrored man in a semi-tractor trailer,
slow in rounding a greased-pad pivot, slow
& hating life, and who with his fingers,
later, will hand me the new *All Girl Anal*
like a wag from a blinking, beaten down dog saying
ain't it a Chinese Fire Drill?
which, yes, it is each and every blessed time
so it seems natural.

Sex Fiend Sonnet

Today I'm on the level. I'm not here
to double your *entendre* or your fun,
though, trouble is, trouble (both *ex-* and *in-*)
tends, virus-wise, to spread out everywhere.

And so you giggle, while I, chaste as a Pope,
dream of his underling's sweet underthings.
There, what sets me off, see, is synechdoche,
the whole-conjuring part. *What whole? or whose?*

Remove a letter, an orgy ensues—hat, hole, hose.
And when I say *artichoke* need I say more?
Trouble was, I was just a guy until
I fit a profile. Today I'm on the level:

I'm not here, though sure as hell somewhere I'm
the lowest of the low. The wreck I've caused I am.

Desperate Message

Exigencies of the greenback hold,
and keep holding forth like a fist.
Money talks, and poetry gets the old
boot in the pants—nothing new in that,
nothing new here under the sun;
the heart constant, tautological,
fueled by an argument it can't win,
stays after hours, continues the tutorial:
to whom, to whom . . . To what does one owe
this soft insistence, this steady method?
The lights are on, but nobody's home.
Is that what you are, an old joke, undismayed?
Pick yourself off the pavement—listen,
this is a road—it's a mountain you need.

G r a v e y a r d   S h i f t

By the light of the Last Days—
amber, a bit theatrical, a vacant lot light,

snowfall muffling the high-volt hum
transformers make zapping snowflakes

to Kingdom Come, somewhere off the interstate
outside Romeoville, Illinois—

the proof of which can be heard —
a ringing noise in the ear

louder and louder until it's a taxi horn
stuck & echoing off the bay doors—

by those who would only listen —
waking the attack dogs out back

for the octodecillionth time,
the guy, Mahmood, begging for wire cutters—

these back-sliding days are numbered —
and, sadly, I have no wire cutters,

but I point him down the road
to the orange revolving ball—

Of the inferno, the grand enveloping fire —
where I think they'll have some wire cutters—

I can only say I hope you are ready —
The last few hours the worst,

mostly cops, a few drunks veering off the road—
to rise into the rapture—

a knocking sound, the furnace,
the day-shift guys clocking in—

whereafter, emptiness,
while the rest rise to greet the day.

Empire Burlesque

The president is pacing in his room—
order out, order in? Snowfall clobbers the capital.
There is no kingdom in our kingdom of the moon.

All things to all and everyone—
O, my fever dream, my translucent girl . . .
The president is pacing in his room.

Troubles mount and shift, of course, and soon
amid the drift we'll sound like keening spaniels—
"There's no *kingdom* in our kingdom of the moon."

Friends, Romans. . . . embrace the chain of command,
eternity . . . whatever's left—a sky like mother-of-pearl,
a president pacing in his room.

The storm unleashed, the Pope on hold, an idea come—
"Quick, get a pencil.". . ."Sir?". . . He scribbles
all there is—*no kingdom in our kingdom of the moon . . .*

And the rest, that brilliant, ferocious question
beneath a sky like hammered steel? No matter.
The president is pacing in his room.
There is no kingdom in our kingdom of the moon.

Saint Monday

She was what they call petite.
She was small, okay?
She was tiny—on her days off I carefully

placed her in my shirt pocket
and walked magically to the office,
where she'd whisper things and help me with my spelling.

Mondays I'd take her to lunch
& give her my wry tilt of the head
which meant *you should eat more.*

There was nothing we wouldn't do
except dance, which looked foolish
and made me very bitter at times.

But a man knows what he wants,
and so too did a woman, once—

"I've got something for you," she said
into my ear, as I looked out the window,
the world for the first time whole.

Postcards and
Joseph Cornell

The smart money spent the summer—
and left the poorer relatives agape,
and sent the change in ash and oak,
post-marked, *laughs galore in Smoky Mountains,*

& *sea shore where she sold her shells*
& other things. The genre's born of envy:
If I were dead I'd write you still,
and come to you, tapping the ceiling fan.

You'd freeze despite the heat, stock still,
and there I'd have you 'till you flicked the switch.
and that would be my message—*click—*
a matchbook, a toothpick, a lipstick laid

just so—to stay put, a brick in a box,
momento mori-wise—so a young man
shuffled the deck again, and a dead hand,
it seems, arranges things while we sleep.

Bad Dates, an Excerpt from the Anthology

Our table: round, small, chest-high. Sunset atop a huge, monolithic, canyon-sized red rock pinnacle, the kind used for car commercials. Behind me, a straight, six-hundred foot drop to the desert floor; behind her a straight, six-hundred foot drop to the desert floor: it's one of those theme restaurants. "I think I'm going crazy," she says, as if considering something from the menu—only there's no menu, the afternoon thermals rushing from the valley floor having blown every-thing away in a tumult of dry heat and sage, wind flapping loudly like a sheet snapping at your ear, menus, table cloth, little boat-shaped folded napkins, silverware and condiments, all of it gone.

We compare impact craters, ring fingers, resumes.

The waiter returns. "Can I get you something else?"
"Yes, yes—bring us lots of something else."

"I think I've caught something incurable," she says.
"My eyes look about the cruel, mean world, undismayed!" I yodel.

Tea arrives.

"Hey look at those two," she says. Our hands are gesturing salaciously toward one another and now combine and intertwine in the variety of obscene, fornicatory "little man, little woman" positions of yore.

We view this from a satellite in geosynchronous orbit fifty miles above our table.

Together we have been locating lithium abundances in 29 cool car-bon stars. Procedure: stare intently across the room at one another. Between times, contemplate the funny staying power of love.

E r o s i o n

They are small and flat, riverbed stones
that can hardly believe the long journey,
the grand lapidary of wind and water,
has led them, finally,
to a snug fit in the soft delta
of the palm, to be rubbed and rubbed again
in the recesses of the pocket.
They are unlikely companions, one polished,
the product of some refinement,
tear-shaped and, it seems, a bit frail,
the other, an earnest little piece of a mountain,
cut and tumbled from the scree one day,
a rock *nouveau*, a rock's rock.

There is justice in the world,
and the rocks are quite prepared
to ride it out in this bag of notions,
forever amongst car keys, chapstick,
an occasional ticket stub—
because if it weren't here,
it would be as it is elsewhere:

the world grinding itself to dust.

Desperate Message

Their hands have found in each other
the impossibility of bodies.
They gather what they can.
Here, and here, in the tangled turn,
in the soft, suede taper of the neck,
in desire they are wise
to the body's overflowing reticence:
nothing is ever enough, is the joke
that keeps giving itself to us,
the air calm, the trees lime-colored,
the hands, like tourists without visas,
cameras without film, busily, purposefully,
taking picture after picture after picture.

Tiny Histories

This is what we have:
we have endurance,

we have the eloquent example
of numbers: *the dinosaurs lived*

one-hundred-and-fifty million years,
and we have our tiny histories,

which seem real enough: the daily
frictions in general, your

incessant typing in particular.
These small things bring us close

to a story even we know the end of.
Sometimes we sit, waiting to be sad,

because it's always difficult,
even when it's easy. I know.

I had to spoof one or two demons
just to get here, to this familiar bed,

to you: we have at times,
this momentum only, this current

which pulls us toward one another, flush
with oblivion.

THREE

Notes and Elegies

A u g u r y

The flight of birds is persuasive,
the weight of sheer numbers
brought to bear, as though a conversation
about you is taking place
in which true things are said among many
in another language—you cannot connect.
Wave upon wave fly from the trees,
forming one long, colonous path
that dips and climbs over each cube,
each slant surface of roof or shed,
a multitude of wings headed inland, moving
away from here, away from where you stand,
now—this part of the past.

Eternity, a List

In the heat of the afternoon, marigolds.
Someone slips out the back door in sandals.

Cars parked on a side street, they know,
and the doppler drone of an airplane diminishing

into the blue bowl—everything
speaks of it—

in the bedroom, a collection of briefcases.
Next to the shoe rack, rows of ties,

the whole of my father rendered an immaculate,
preposterously small boxful of ash,

a last gesture of economy—elemental and strange,
the body's answer to the flame:

no cause, no cause . . .
Across the bay, a freighter's long vowel,

the horizon, asking nothing, gives and gives,
with each slow roll of the sea rail, nothing.

W i f e

You suffered, instead—
long life, three sons, the last a surprise,

and a fourth,
old Dad, who died—

this the brief history of him:
and then, and then, and then—

broke upon us and we awoke
and you awoke

that morning,
and our grief broke, ebbed,

and you tried, I think,
for the first time,

to wear that last year thin—
and then—you followed him.

Player Piano
(Crows at Dusk)

Here's the blank page set in motion—
each note a dot in the sky.
Here they come in echelons across the sky.
Soon too her music will come,
a little number, *in-the-Ram-halve-cours-yronne*
or whatever. The music will come, I say,
though there's no one in the chair today.
No one? All's well, then, and perfection
is a ringing in the ear. Let's see: *rotting teeth,*
rotting dear, rotting mom, I feel so queer.
There, she's at her favorite tune, slowly now,
over that bumpy passage. *Crows, being birds, have no teeth . . .*
So I'd tease her from the weird
part—if only I could impart this to the ground.

Variation on the Theme
of Disappearance

I

My mother is a doorbell,
　　　　　my father a set

of green, porcelain saki
　　　　　glasses—they call the technique raku,

the purposeful
　　　　　cracking of the beautiful.

The technique says
　　　　　it is possible to believe

in green, porcelain saki glasses—
　　　　　they are sufficient.

Beyond this
　　　　　they are silent.

II

　　　　　Did they seem

rare to a man and a woman,
　　　　　from Cody, and from Bloomfield,

an Airforce commission under his belt,
　　　　　sent to Japan

to help make *things*
        work again—did he bargain

for them, for these—
        did she say, *honey, please.*

then a few bows
        of the head of the craftsman?

III

Saturdays, a Japanese man came onto base
        to wash the officer's cars.

I don't know how many times I sat
        watching him

twist the chamois to get the water out,
        twist it tight as a rope in the hands,

or a chicken's neck.
        He never spoke a word, nor did I.

Saturdays were egg days,
        which meant a drive off base,

into the countryside,
        always to the same roadside barn,

the place smelling of cardboard,
        chalk and straw,

always a sprinkle of rain,
        always a little breeze, it seemed—

IV

or a fog down from the mountainside,
                        as in a living room's silk tryptich—

a blonde, rural scene,
                        a gash in the lower left,

a child's fuck-up,
                        but still,

—in the barnyard, the hen's polite commentary
                        a kind of clockwork

the ear grew accustomed to,
                        like background noise,

as one came to know, off base or on,
                        the balance

of eggs traded for yen, always,
                        was silence.

V

I was small
                        when the transistor was big.

I was learning the difference
                        between *bib* and *did*.

Where had the war gone, after all?
                        You couldn't find it

in Tachikawa AFB, 1963,
          not at Yamato High,

where the Beachboys ruled,
          where you could letter in Judo,

like Shields Jones, like Tim Lapointe—
          the technique says *half-tone*

on glossy—they are laying lay-ups,
          in a gym the size of an air hanger

because it *is* an air hanger—
          after practice, my brother says,

over the phone,
          because I've asked him,

we'd sneak out onto the tarmac.
          You'd have to watch it

or be blown flat by the prop-blast.
          A rare shot—

five guys in gym trunks, grinning,
          leaning into nothing, almost

horizontal, as the great plane
          bellies its way out of sight—

the technique says
          they will not disappear.

which is different from *can you believe it?*
          I can't believe half of what he says.

VI

I've been walking around all day
                          saying the word *Mary*

because I've just met a woman named Mary.
                          This won't do, this won't do at all.

This is terrible.
                          Saturdays I take the car

down to the strip.
                          They've got a car wash there.

You've got to wash your car
                          because of the salt,

and, against the drift of things,
                          especially if it's sunny

and the power wand
                          is working right,

Mary, it makes me feel
                          like a citizen of something.

This is terrible—
                          this Burger King on the left

that Donut Haus on the right—
                          it's background noise, all of it,

against the inglorious drift of things,
                          (two oaks in full leaf

toss the old song across the lot, the sky
                    a high, inverted prairie fire)

And if you were to ask about them,
                    my mother and father,

about Japan, how it was—
                    if I held up a pair of green

porcelain saki glasses,
                    would both of us laugh

to break the silence,
                    the bad *haiku*

—that would be terrible.
                    That won't do.

Desperate Message

Not the end of the world,
but a mouthful of salt water
sends you shuttling against the slope,
against the difficult pull of the surf.
Not the buried wish, rocketed forth, at last,
but seven sleek mackerel,
together in a flash before your eyes,
leap from their pursuer.
No private end, no melodrama
by cartridge or clip, the fine smell of bluing,
the slip of the knot that stops the neck—
none of that. Against the coast line, that roar
is the ocean's steady method,
hammering the pinnacles with a vengeance
that knows nothing is ever finished,
neither erosion, nor hope,
nor the endless harvest of speech.

Winter Solstice

I

How difficult it is to bring oneself back to love,
for instance.

II

The heart gutted, renovated,
an efficiency apartment with all the little gizmos
that signal the move from Peyton Place to complacent place.

III

The idea of love reading like a text
on sidereal time or the astronomical unit,
the distances too great, the facts facts.

IV

And yet, the wind—
little scraps of it
blown flat against the schoolyard fence,
school girls trying
to out-shout the gusts,

V

a dry, Chinook wind,
and the deepening green dusk,

VI

and the cantilevered flagrancies
of the pigeons,
rising in a rush to round the plaza,
to circle the square—

VII

birds (by the idiot bus-load)

VIII

and Canada geese, well-travelled, impeccably dressed.
What a thing to be called "Goose."
You are sensible, and shy away from my hand,
murmuring something in *goose*—
It's true, I *do* have some other place to be,
but I'll watch, for a while, anyway—
your serious business.

IX

To arrive like this,
from some distance, from above the buildings,
above the stadium, above the flags snapping in the breeze,
and above that, above the possible,
to arrive from that into the slant-light and tremor
of this squeaky, well-tended
patch of turf, to arrive severally,
in convincing numbers—but not for you, no,
their heads poised on dark stems,
the whole lot of them like strolling statuary,

but not for you—none of it
merely for you.

X

The caption of this tableau reads:
Mourner with ham sandwich observing geese.
Above him, Grief and Happiness assume their rightful spots

among the gargoyles.

XI

Who knows the world's irony as I do,
knows the Renton freeway exit, and the main drag
up Cemetery Road and the turn into the parking lot,
and the walk through the stilled grounds
by a plot of perennially trampled grass
with a modest plaque bearing an engraved electric guitar,
and, beneath, the words *James "Jimi" Hendrix*—that way
also leads to a few hundred other plaques—
and to two in particular—
who, while on this earth could never, ever stand that guitar.

XII

But that's the way it goes, isn't it—
comic touching tragic—geese on parade,
squabbling among the grave stones.

Two rectangles of wet marble—

what an angle
you make with each other as
you lie there in contemplation.

XIII

But all your work leads away from arrival—
(all is distraction, digression, the weather changeable).
What you want is the brick-work in the sun,
warm against your palm—
what you want is to push
against the simple brick,
the one-way door, the gathering of things into themselves
that pushes back with equal force,

that won't budge,
now, and now—

until with the confidence of objects you walk the cobblestones,
delivered of another era,

XIV

and the wind shifts, plausibly,
and the geese softly shovel gravel into their beaks.

Notes

"Death of the Cabaret Hegel" is for Stephen Thomas, who openly perpetrated a reading and performance series in the old Buffalo Shoe Factory, Seattle, Washington, from November, 1984, to February, 1988, in contravention of the usual sumptuary laws. The factory was home to a number of artists and writers but was replaced by a freeway interchange. Many thanks to Peter Stitt, editor of the *Gettysburg Review*, for publishing this, in its entirety, under the title "Seattle Sequence."

"Villanelle *Fin De Siecle*." The scene involves an installation by Ann Hamilton entitled *Tropos*.

"Bad Dates, an Excerpt from the Anthology." For peak performance, listen to Henry Mancini's "Mr. Lucky" (*Henry Mancini/A Legendary Performer*, RCA 07863/51843-2) while reading this poem.

Eternity, a List. "No cause, no cause. . ."—Cordelia loves her father, assures him she harbors no grievance, or cause, against him, *King Lear* (IV.iv.75).

"Winter Solstice" transcribes William Carlos Williams' "January Morning" into a slightly different key.